YOGA
AND
MYSTICISM

By *Swami Prabhavananda*

ORIGINAL WORKS
Vedic Religion and Philosophy
The Eternal Companion
The Spiritual Heritage of India (with Frederick Manchester)
Sermon on the Mount According to Vedanta
Religion in Practice

TRANSLATIONS
Bhagavad-Gita (with Christopher Isherwood)
The Upanishads (with Frederick Manchester)
Wisdom of God
Crest-Jewel of Discrimination (with Christopher Isherwood)
How to Know God (with Christopher Isherwood)
Swami Premananda: Teachings and Reminiscences

OTHER
What Is Religion? (record)

YOGA

AND

MYSTICISM

SWAMI PRABHAVANANDA

Vedanta Press
HOLLYWOOD, CALIFORNIA

If you wish to learn in greater detail about the
teachings contained in this book, write to the
Secretary, Vedanta Society of Southern California, 1946 Vedanta Place, Hollywood, CA
90068-3996.

Contents

Peace and Holiness   7

Yoga—True and False   17

Mysticism—True and False   30

Know Thy Self   40

Faith   55

Peace and Holiness

ALTHOUGH there are many people perhaps who are not drawn to a life of holiness, it would seem that nearly all people search for peace—whether they are believers, agnostics, or even atheists. Only they do not know where to find it, or how to find it. But we cannot blame them for that. If I were permitted to do so, I should blame God, because it is said that "God created the senses outgoing"; therefore, men cannot help themselves. Their senses are always involved in the external. And so when they seek religion, when they seek God, they think they can find him with their senses; therefore, they seek peace outside of themselves. Men want to find peace and harmony in the world. For example, they feel that if there is no war, there will be peace. They do not remember, however, that there have been times when there has been no war. Did men then find peace? Many of us have witnessed two great world wars, wars fought to end all wars, and we are witnessing still another conflict.

Let me state that I am neither for war nor against it, because there is war, chaos, and conflict always in the world. My own feeling, as one of your great presidents once said, is that "patriotism is not enough." My ideal is to have one mankind, one world. It is for all mankind to live in peace and harmony, not necessarily by thinking the same thoughts, nor by believing in the same way. Let each individual, let each nation keep its individuality; and at the same time, let all people learn to live in harmony and peace. That would be my idea of a Utopia. In my heart of hearts, however, I do not believe this can happen. But I do wish it would. As Swami Vivekananda once said: "What is this world but a dog's curly tail; you straighten it and the next moment it curls again." That is the nature of the world. The ideal of a millennium, though ideally attractive, is not possible.

Suppose there is only light. Can we know what light is without comparing it with darkness? Suppose there is only good (and I know of no one who can define it). Could you then possibly see everything as "good"? For how can we recognize good unless we contrast it to evil? These are the pairs of opposites that have to exist in the world so long as there is this world. When there is unification, a total oneness, the world as we know it will disappear. So, in the very midst of the pairs of opposites, we must learn to find peace and harmony in our own individual lives.

Now, as I said earlier, if there is no war, do you think there will be peace? Consider your own family. Are you at peace? Do you live in harmony with one another? Life would be very dull, would it not, if you didn't fight occasionally! Leaving aside nations or families, consider yourself as an individual. Are you at peace *within* yourself? Or is there not some conflict there? Yes, that is human nature. But that does not mean that our human nature will endure or must endure always. Man must eventually recognize his own divinity—because that is his true nature.

IN THIS connection, let me quote the great American philosopher, Ralph Waldo Emerson. He said:

> There are two laws discrete
> Not reconciled;
> Law for man, and law for things.
> The last builds town and fleet,
> But it runs wild
> And doth the man unking.

How very true this is, especially today. We have built towns and fleets, and we have learned how to destroy all mankind. Does that bring us peace?

The *Bhagavad-Gita* begins on a battlefield. The first chapter describes the preparations for battle between two armies. We may also regard this as a conflict occurring within our own selves—our own human bodies. In this body, which may be called the "field of holiness" because it is the temple of God, there is a battle going on. Everyone has to go through such a fight, through that battle within himself. There are two forces existing in us, good and evil, and there is eternal conflict between them. One great philosopher of India described two "currents," as it were, in an ordinary person; one is a surface current, and the other, an undercurrent. The surface current flows through life, seeking pleasures and the possession of external objects. But the undercurrent flows towards God, freedom, and peace. Much later, the great psychologist Sigmund Freud spoke of a conflict in man between two wills—the will to live and the will to die. He pointed out that although nobody can overcome the will to die, it is possible to conquer the will to live.

Likewise, the undercurrent will prevail in the end. No one will be lost. That undercurrent, that current which flows toward God and freedom and peace will

9

prevail, and each one of us will ultimately reach the kingdom of Self, the kingdom of God.

There was once a king who was suffering from amnesia. Because of the illness, he forgot that he was king; he carried the search throughout his kingdom. At long last he came to his minister, and asked him: "Where is the king?" The minister pointed to him, and said, "You are the king." In the same way, we have forgotten our real nature. This condition of suffering is a kind of sleep. We have to awake from this sleep. We have to become a Buddha, "The Awakened One." We must become Christs and Buddhas; these are the states to be attained by each individual. Christhood is not limited to Jesus. Buddhahood is not limited to Buddha. It is man's true nature.

Take, for instance, the idea of evolution. In evolution there is nothing superadded. What is already involved becomes evolved. In the highest manifestation, we see the highest evolution, a Christ or a Buddha, because Christhood or Buddhahood is involved in every one of us. As Swami Vivekananda once said—and it really shocked his audience: "The worm that crawls under our feet is the brother of the Nazarene." Many times when he spoke like that several of the audience would walk out on him. One time, his secretary was feeling sad to see people leave while he was speaking. Later Swamiji said, "Why are you so sad? I have emptied entire halls in New York!" No, there is no compromise with truth.

Buddha emphasized four noble truths. First, that there is suffering. This we all must admit. Second, there is a cause to this suffering. Third, that there is a way out of suffering. And lastly, the way is described—the way to peace. These are the four noble truths that Christ as well as Buddha preached.

IN THE Upanishads we read, "There is no happiness in the finite; the Infinite alone is happiness." In this connection let me quote the great Western philosopher Spinoza:

For the things which men do judge, by their actions, to be the highest good are riches, fame, or sensual pleasure. Of these, the last is followed by satiety and repentance. The other two are never satiated. The more we have, the more we want. The love of fame compels us to guide our lives by the opinion of others, but if a thing is not loved, no quarrel will arise concerning it, no sadness will be felt if it perishes nor indeed if another has it; in short, no disturbances of the mind. All these spring from the love of that which passes away. But the love of a thing eternal and infinite fills the mind only with joy, and is unmingled with sadness. Therefore, it is greatly to be desired, and to be sought with all our strength.

And what is that eternal? In the Upanishads, God has been defined as the eternal amongst the noneternals of life, the highest abiding joy in the midst of the fleeting pleasures of life.

There is the charge against oriental religions that they are pessimistic, that they negate life and affirm suffering. But I would say all religions at the start are pessimistic. Did not St. Paul say: "The whole creation has been groaning in travail together until now, and not only the creation, but we ourselves, who are the first fruits of the spirit, groan immensely as we wait for adoption as sons." Let me also add here the words of a great Christian mystic, Angelus Silesius, who said: "Christ may be born a thousand times in Bethlehem, but until He is born anew in your own heart you will remain forever forlorn." An even greater man than these, Jesus himself, told us that "in the world ye shall have tribulations." Isn't that pessimistic? But he added in comforting assurance to troubled hearts: "But be of good cheer; I have overcome the world."

That is the thing to do. Like Christ, we have to overcome the world. And where is this world? In ourselves. Once, the great philosopher Shankara was asked: "By whom has the world been conquered?" His answer was: "By him who has conquered his own mind." So the world is in our own mind. It is that world we must conquer.

Again let me quote Jesus: "Peace I leave with you, my peace I give unto you: not as the world giveth, give I unto you. Let not your heart be troubled, neither let it be afraid." Buddha taught the same truth, that there is a way to peace. And it is found also in the Upanishadic statement we have just quoted, that "the Infinite alone is happiness." But this peace is, as St. Paul remarked, something "that passeth understanding."

"Glory to God in the highest, and on earth peace among men with whom He is pleased." There *is* peace amongst men with whom he is pleased. Then, is he pleased with some and displeased with others? No. But, naturally, if one loves God, he is very much pleased. For everybody seeks love, even God! And so God is pleased when one loves him. In the Gita it is said: "To love God is to know him." And remember the two commandments found in the Old Testament, which were repeated by Jesus? "Love the Lord thy God with all thy heart, with all thy strength, with all thy mind, and with all thy soul." And "Love thy neighbour as thy Self." Today, unfortunately, they speak not of loving, but of *helping* mankind. That is religion today. The commandments have been forgotten.

Now at this point I must remind you that we must learn this truth—that ultimate Reality (call it God or

Brahman or Allah or Christ)—is not merely to be be-
lieved in, is not a mere hypothesis, but a soul-experi-
ence. We have to experience *That* within ourselves.
From the Vedic times up to this present day, in Buddha,
Christ, and Ramakrishna, we find an emphasis on realizing Truth for ourselves. In the Vedas we read: "I
have known that truth; having realized it, I have gone
beyond darkness." Then the seer continues: "You also,
knowing that truth will attain to immortality." He
doesn't simply say, "Believe me." He knows that when
a man is hungry, his appetite will not be satisfied by
someone else eating for him. Can we obtain greater en-
joyment by seeing only a painting of the moon and not
the real moon? The great philosopher Shankara pointed
out that scriptures alone are not the authority. A man
may believe in scriptures, but if he is a fool he will remain a fool regardless of how many scriptures he reads.
Scriptures are not the ultimate authority. But your personal experience is. In India, we are not asked if we
have faith, nor only if we believe. People will say:
"What is your *experience* of God?" It is most unfortunate that with the exception of a relatively few mystics,
the Christian world does not understand what is meant
by an experience of God.

The truth is, that experience is *not* within these three
states of consciousness—waking, dreaming, and dreamless sleep. One has to venture beyond, to transcendental,
supersensory consciousness, in order to know spiritual
truth. Western psychologists, for instance, know only
of the three areas of the mind: conscious, subconscious,
and unconscious. But of superconsciousness they
have no knowledge. They refer to the superconscious
experience as "self-hypnosis." If I, who have no
knowledge of science and admit it, begin to talk
on physics—what nonsense that would be! What

would physicists think about such talk? That I do not know what I am talking about, of course. Have these psychiatrists and psychologists ever meditated? Have they ever struggled to find the truth of God? Without making any attempt, without learning even what meditation is, they call it self-hypnosis. To use a colloquial, but very apt, expression, "What cheek!"

IN THIS age, Sri Ramakrishna emphasized the truth that we can see God, that we can talk to him, that we can become one with him. I have met his disciples, those who had had this experience and had realized God. And they, in turn, taught us how to realize God. In the presence of those men, one felt that peace "that passeth understanding." When Swami Vivekananda was in this country he talked with Robert Ingersoll, the well-known, so-called agnostic, and Ingersoll told Swamiji, "If I had been God, I would have made health contagious instead of disease." Swami Vivekananda replied: "Don't you know that health also is contagious?" Just so, peace too is contagious. That is why there is always an emphasis on associating with holy people, so that one also can become holy.

In the words of Jesus: "Blessed are the pure in heart, for they shall see God." They shall see God! What is purity of heart? First, it is discrimination between the eternal and noneternal. And what is eternal? The abiding Reality, God. What proof is there for the existence of God? The only proof is that he can be known and experienced. Logical or scientific proofs will never prove God's reality; he is a matter of *fact*, a fact of experience. A scientist will certainly never believe in data until he tests it. He will then say: "I have conducted so-and-so experiment. Come to my laboratory, conduct your own experiment; see for yourself." In this same way God is proved. Experiment—and experience him for yourself. Buddha, too, emphasized that one must experience the truth through experiment. When we realize that He is the Reality, then He becomes the treasure. For Jesus said: "Where your treasure is, there will your heart be also."

In order that that truth can be realized, the mind must be under complete control. As I already pointed out, we have to overcome this world by conquering our own mind. To quote the words of the Gita:

> Utterly quiet
> Made clean of passion,
> The mind of the yogi
> Knows that Brahman,
> His bliss is the highest.
> Released from evil
> His mind is constant
> In contemplation:
> The way is easy,
> Brahman has touched him,
> That bliss is boundless.

How very true. Brahman, as it were, touches him. You *feel* that grace. The Gita says elsewhere:

The light of a lamp does not flicker in a windless place—that is the simile which describes a yogi of one-pointed mind, who meditates upon the indwelling God.

When through the practice of Yoga, the mind ceases its restless movements, and becomes still, he realizes the Atman, it satisfies him entirely. Then he knows that infinite happiness which can be realized by the purified heart, but is beyond the grasp of the senses.

Now, in this connection, again may I quote to you from the Beatitudes, "Blessed are the peacemakers, for they shall be called the children of God." Let me illustrate this from the life of my Master, Swami

15

Brahmananda. One time in our organization in Benares, various groups of monks had formed cliques, and created disturbances. So the General Secretary of the Order went to inquire, and soon found the guilty ones. He wrote to my Master, Swami Brahmananda, who was then the President of the Order: "If we can expel these guilty ones, then perhaps there will be peace." Maharaj replied immediately, "Don't do anything. I am coming." When he came, he did not ask who was guilty or who was not guilty. He simply gave this one order: "I want all of you boys to come and meditate every day with me." So they came, and they sat and meditated with him every day for a month. He did not say one word about the fight or quarrel. After a month he left, and there was complete peace and harmony and no more trouble. You see, such men are the real peacemakers, for they possess genuine holiness. If there were a few dozen such souls in this age, our world would be blessed. Therefore, it is my plea that each of you grow in holiness and realize peace within yourself. It is through being holy that true peace is achieved and we can become real peacemakers.

Yoga—True and False

IN RECENT years, a great deal of interest has been aroused in this country concerning *yoga*. And, we may be sure, whenever there is a demand for anything, there will be people to meet that demand regardless of whether the article is genuine or spurious. As a result of this present demand, a large number of teachers as well as institutions of yoga have begun to flourish.

But first, what *is* yoga? According to Patanjali, the father of Indian Yoga philosophy, yoga is the method of controlling the vagaries of the mind—to make it one-pointed. In order to understand this better, try to concentrate your mind on an object for any length of time. You will soon see how many distractions begin to arise in it. Patanjali called these distractions "waves on the lake of the mind." The ultimate purpose of controlling the mind, he declared, was to reveal the truth of God, which lies in everyone's heart.

The word "yoga" literally means "union." Similarly, if we examine the English word "religion," we find that its early Latin derivative is *religio*, "to bind again." But to bind with what? With God, who is dwelling within. Through ignorance we have forgotten that we possess this divinity within. Hence, it is the purpose of yoga to reveal it to us. Swami Vivekananda, you will recall, defines religion as the unfoldment of the divinity already within man.

It is also unfortunately true that to a great many people in the West yoga has come to be identified with what in India we call *hatha yoga*, which mainly teaches *asanas* or postures, and *pranayama* or breathing exercises. Of course, as we shall presently see, these are the "limbs" of Patanjali's Yoga. But hatha yoga emphasizes them to the exclusion of everything else. We might compare these postures to various exercises, which, if they are begun when one is young, can be of great benefit to health. They increase one's longevity; therefore, there are many who practice hatha yoga in order to live long and be healthy. Nothing, certainly, is wrong with that. But as Swami Vivekananda once said: "In your country the redwood tree is the most ancient tree in the world, but it still remains a tree."

Now we come to breathing exercises. Let me caution you: they can be very dangerous. Unless properly done, there is a good chance of injuring the brain. And those who practice such breathing without proper supervision can suffer a disease which no known science or doctor can cure. It is impossible, even, for a medical person to diagnose such an illness. I know of one individual who complained to me of constantly experiencing headaches; and though he had gone to a number of doctors, they were unable to do anything for him. I asked him, "Have you been practicing breathing exercises?"

"Yes," he said, "I have."

At once I knew the source of his problem.

I know of one other case. Shortly before I left India to come to the United States, I had known a young boy of perhaps sixteen or seventeen years of age who had begun to practice hatha yoga. When I returned to India after an absence of some thirteen years, I visited one of our centers. While sitting on the porch talking to a swami, I happened to notice a young person in the distance. He was acting very strangely. He would prostrate fully on the ground, rise to full height, then repeat the performance—over and over again. The swami said that he had lost his mind. When the fellow approached me I was amazed to see that he still looked the same as when I knew him thirteen years ago! So it was true: certain exercises did keep one youthful. Yet how costly! Then he showed me various exercises, many of which I knew to be difficult to master. In jest, I told him, "You should go to America. There you will make millions." Unfortunately, he took me seriously, and even followed me to Benares, presumably with the hope that I would indeed take him to the United States. Finally, however, he became so unmanageable that he had to be confined.

Another unfortunate characteristic of hatha yoga is that the mind becomes much attached to the body. Health is certainly important, but if too much attention is paid to the body spiritual growth can be greatly hindered. *The ideal, we must remember, is to completely forget the body; ignorance is identification with the body.* No spiritual experience can come to us until we are completely oblivious of the body's existence; in fact, until we are completely oblivious of the world's existence. Thus, Sri Ramakrishna said that it is best to avoid hatha yoga because of the attention it requires we pay to the body and its obstruction to spiritual advancement. As regards breathing exercises, I know that Sri Ramakrishna, Holy Mother, and all the disciples of Ramakrishna have warned us again and again not to practice them.

THERE also exists another dangerously false idea about yoga. Some teachers have recently been speaking about meditation, which, of course, is the very core and central truth of spiritual life. Real meditation is real yoga. But the kind of meditation to which these teachers refer has no real basis, but is, more than anything, pure confusion. They point out meditation to be simple and easy, demanding hardly any sacrifice or self-restraint. Continue to live as you have been living, they tell us, it doesn't really matter. Is it any wonder then they have attracted a large number of followers!

Let me quote one of them from a recent issue of a popular American magazine: "To qualify as a meditator, a prospective convert needs no preparation, no intellectual background; [meditation] requires no repudiation of the past, and no promise to behave in the future."

Let me again quote this same "yogi" concerning meditation. He says: "[In meditation] a man can make daily contact with the aspects of his own being."

Wonderful! But can we do it? Let me finish his remark: "...without any effort or concentration." How easy he makes it sound for us! But in the next paragraph he contradicts himself by describing meditation as "the transference of attention..." (Note that he avoids the word concentration!) "from the gross state of thought to the subtle state, until the source of thought is reached and the mind transcends the source." These are indeed high-sounding words—and one wonders what they mean. It appears to be so simple and easy to attain transcendental bliss. "You need not practice any dispassion or nonattachment to worldliness." In other words, he says, we do not have to give up any of our old habits or our normal or abnormal ways of living. Eat, drink, and make merry, practice yoga, and attain transcendental bliss!

There is another false idea of yoga which has become popular. It states that to make our minds quiet we must make them blank. It would seem the easiest way of doing this would be to simply ask a friend to strike us over the head! Or we might drug ourselves and thereby sleep so profoundly that not even dreams would invade our minds. But from nothing can come only nothing, and if one goes into such a state a fool, he will come out of it a fool.

Still another misconception about meditation is that it involves the contemplation of some subject, say a poem by Wordsworth, from which various thoughts and ideas are expected to emerge. This is the type of definition of meditation which we find in the dictionary; but as we shall discover meditation is anything but that. It is not many-pointed, but one-pointed, and requires concentration as its first requisite.

LET US turn now to what we might term "true yoga." From the lips of Sri Krishna, the Lord of yogis, issued these words in the *Bhagavad-Gita*: "Patiently, little by little, a man must free himself from all mental distractions, with the aid of the intelligent will."

> Utterly quiet,
> Made clean of passion,
> The mind of the yogi
> Knows that Brahman;
>
> Released from evil,
> His mind is constant
> In contemplation:

The way is easy,
Brahman has touched him;
That bliss is boundless.

Mark these words: "His mind is constant in contemplation: the way is easy, Brahman has touched him." One actually does feel the touch of God, and "that bliss is boundless."

There was one great spiritual aspirant who was aware of the difficulty that arises in the practice of concentration and meditation. This was Arjuna the warrior, Sri Krishna's disciple and constant companion. Arjuna said to Krishna: "You describe this yoga as a life of union with Brahman. But I do not see how this can be permanent. The mind is so very restless. Truly I think the wind is no wilder."

Krishna's response is truly wonderful. "Yes, Arjuna, the mind is restless, no doubt, and hard to subdue. But it can be brought under control by constant practice, and by the exercise of dispassion. Certainly, if a man has no control over his ego, he will find this yoga difficult to master. But a self-controlled man can master it if he struggles hard, and uses the right means."

Before we discuss these "right means" let us study two interesting parables by Sri Ramakrishna. The first is the story of a farmer whose fields were dry and who found it necessary to water them throughout the night. But when day broke, and he looked out over the fields, he noticed they were still dry. The water had escaped through holes in the walls of the channel. In the same way, unless we conserve ourselves through self-control, the mind will remain restless. Our spiritual energy will escape through the holes of the senses.

Another story of Ramakrishna's concerns some drunkards who discovered a boat one dark night and after getting inside it began to row. They rowed all night. But when dawn broke they discovered that they had gone nowhere. They had forgotten to take up the anchor. Therefore, in order to succeed in spiritual life, we must learn how to direct our energies and not waste them fruitlessly.

MEDITATION is the means to one-pointedness and a primary discipline of yoga. The Sanskrit *dhyana* is translated as meditation, although this is not entirely accurate, for dhyana is a difficult word to translate. In Japan, dhyana has come to have something of the same meaning as *Zen*. Zen Buddhism emphasizes meditation, as you might know. I have had the pleasure of knowing one great Zen scholar, Dr. D. T. Suzuki. Once I asked Dr. Suzuki: "Doctor, don't you believe in spiritual disciplines and meditation?"

"Of course we do," he answered.

Then I told him that one of his disciples, who was a great student of his writings, was preaching that it was not necessary to practice any disciplines.

"I wish I could burn all my books," Dr. Suzuki said with a sigh.

Real meditation means that there must be a flow of thought directed toward an ideal, the ideal of God, *without any break in continuity*. You see, most of us can't meditate, but we can concentrate, if only for a short time, and through the practice of concentration we reach a stage where we begin to meditate; that is, where there is no break in our thought. The illustration has been given of oil being poured from one vessel to another without any break in the flow of the liquid. In order for us to reach this stage in our meditation we must create an interest in God; that interest causes us to continue thinking about God until love grows within; without love, meditation is not possible.

Let us see what Sri Krishna says in the Gita:

> Though a man be soiled
> With the sins of a lifetime,
> Let him but love me,
> Rightly resolved,
> In utter devotion:
> I see no sinner,
> That man is holy.
> Holiness soon
> Shall refashion his nature
> To peace eternal;
> O son of Kunti,
> Of this be certain:
> The man that loves me
> He shall not perish.

And in the Bible, we find the first commandment to be: "Love the Lord thy God with all thy heart, with all thy soul, with all thy strength and with all thy mind."

In order to achieve this state of meditation we must practice spiritual disciplines, and the main principle behind these disciplines is purity of heart. But in order for such purity of heart to arise in us, we must be able to discriminate between the real and the unreal; to realize that today everything is, tomorrow it is not. Of course, this does not mean that we must give up all our possessions and live in the woods! The real ideal of dispassion and nonattachment is to cover everything with the presence of God. I see you before me. But what is that *you*? None other than Brahman or God—in each one of us. It is He we must learn to see. He we must learn to love. We must love each and every one, all of mankind. How is this possible? By seeing that one Divinity, that one Reality existing everywhere.

We should remember, however, that before such

discrimination and love can arise we must develop a desire for God. How many really want God? How many are struggling for the knowledge of God?

WE HAVE mentioned earlier the philosophy of Patanjali; now let us examine the eight "limbs" or parts of his Yoga system. The first limb is called *yama*. Yama consists in abstention from hurting others, from falsehood, theft, incontinence, and from greed in thought, word, and deed. Let us try to understand what this means. "Abstention from hurting others" means that we must not cause pain to any living soul, nor must we think such thoughts. The positive aspect of this discipline is to see the one Reality, God, in every being. Love your husband, love your wife and your children; serve them, but know that you are serving God in them. Thus it is said in Yoga philosophy: "When a man has been steadfast in his abstention from hurting others, then all creatures will cease to feel enmity in his presence." You see, people say, "Oh, he thinks badly of me. He hurts me." We always complain that *others* cause our troubles.

In this connection, let me tell you one example of how in the presence of a holy man even a wild beast loses its savageness and becomes calm. Swami Brahmananda, my Master, was once walking with two of us down the road near our monastery. Suddenly we heard a cry: "Get out of the way! Get out of the way! A mad bull is coming!" In order to protect our master, both of us stepped in front of him to face the charging bull. But Maharaj suddenly grabbed both of us (and though he was then an old man, we were like feathers to him!) and thrust us behind him. He simply stood there and stared directly at the charging bull. Then an amazing thing happened. The bull almost at

25

once came to a halt directly in front of us, shook its head, and quietly trotted off.

And regarding truthfulness, Maharaj told us: "Tell the truth, but never a harsh truth." Never have malice in your heart for anyone.

Next, Patanjali mentions abstention from theft. Although nobody would call us common thieves, we are, according to Patanjali, thieves in a certain respect. Everything in this world really belongs to God, yet don't we label this "mine" and that "yours"? You say you have earned something. But does it belong to you? Are you not, in a sense, constantly stealing from God or from nature? Patanjali does not ask us to be beggars or give away all we own; but instead consider ourselves trustees. Do not own anything, for when you possess something, that thing will possess you. Then you are bound!

Next, we are asked to abstain from incontinence, which means chastity in word, thought, and deed. Perhaps one remark is suitable here. Married couples are considered chaste if they remain faithful to one another; but the spiritual teacher is expected to abstain totally from sexual activity in order to store his energy, that he might give truth to others. All of these, of course, are ethical virtues which are taught by every religion in the world. And, in addition to these ethics, we are asked to undergo certain regular practices which serve to cleanse us, to purify us. These should become habitual with us. What is man, after all, but a bundle of habits? We can remold our character by creating a new bundle of habits. These habits are purity, both physical and mental, contentment, austerity, study, and devotion or surrender to God. This is the second limb, called *niyama*.

Purity is both inner and outer. Of course, physical

purity is relatively simple; after all, we have to bathe! But even more important than physical cleanliness is purity of mind. My master taught us this truth: "When you sit for meditation, try to feel that you are bathed in the presence of God. You have become pure. Think yourself pure." When I was a young boy, I remember reading in a book that one should repeat to oneself: "You are pure. You are pure. You are pure." Sri Ramakrishna used to say that the wretch who says he is a sinner, a sinner becomes. Of course, we all make mistakes. But chant the name of the Lord and feel that you have become pure; then do not repeat the mistake. And from this purity comes cheerfulness, the power of concentration, control of the passions, and a general fitness for the vision of God. Such is the power of purity.

CONTENTMENT is the next habit we must develop. Contentment means our ability to maintain inner poise—even in the midst of the opposites of life. So long as we live in this world there will be a mixture of happiness and sorrow. There is heat and cold; pleasure and pain; birth and death. But in the midst of these opposites we must hold on to the pillar of God and maintain calmness and poise.

Next is austerity, which is of three kinds: austerity of the body, of speech, and of mind. The Gita defines austerity in this way:

Reverence for the seers, the teachers and sages; straightforwardness, harmlessness, physical cleanliness; these are the virtues whose practice is called austerity of the body. To speak without ever causing pain to another, to be truthful, to say always what is kind and beneficial, and to study the scriptures regularly: this practice is called austerity of speech. The practice of serenity, sympathy, and integrity of motive is called austerity of mind.

Following austerity is study. By study is meant chanting the name of the Lord, repeating your *mantra*. That is the highest study.

Next, we must surrender the fruits of our actions to God. Each day, as you finish your work, think of God and surrender everything to him.

The next limb is *asana* or posture. The Gita speaks of the correct posture for meditation: "Motionless, with the body, head, and neck held erect...." Swamiji has pointed out this steadiness of posture comes to one who meditates on the presence of the all-pervading Existence. In the *Brahma Sutras*, the meditator is compared to the immovable earth. While he is concentrating, the yogi is beyond the law of place. Worship should be performed wherever the mind is concentrated, says this scripture.

Following asana is *pranayama* or control of the vital energy. One method for controlling the *prana* is through concentration. Breathing exercises, as we have mentioned earlier, are discouraged.

Next we come to *pratyahara* or detachment of the mind from objects of sense by not allowing the mind to join itself to the organs of sense—the centers of perception. There is a beautiful passage in the Gita which says: "The tortoise can draw in its legs/The seer can draw in his senses./I call him illumined."

Swami Vivekananda has given us a fine lesson on how to detach ourselves from the sense organs. He writes:

The first lesson is to sit for some time, and let the mind run on. The mind is bubbling up all the time; it is like the monkey jumping about. Let the monkey jump as much as he can, simply wait and watch; knowledge is power, says the proverb, and that is true; until you know what the mind is doing, you cannot control it. Give it the rein. Many

hideous thoughts may come into it, you will be astonished
that it was possible for you to think such thoughts, but
you will find that each day the mind's vagaries are becoming
fewer, and less violent; that each day it is becoming calmer.
In the first few months, you will find that the mind will have
a great many thoughts; later you will find that they have
somewhat decreased, and in a few more months you will
find they are fewer and fewer, until at last the mind will be
under perfect control. But we must patiently practice
every day.

The sixth limb is called *dharana*, i.e. concentration
or holding the mind in one of the centers of spiritual
consciousness in the body. Or we may fix the mind on
some divine form outside or inside the body—which-
ever is simplest. If you begin to think of Him outside,
gradually bring Him inside. Of course, here again there
is no uniform rule for everyone; temperaments differ
and so must the teaching. That is why you need the
help of a *guru*.

The seventh limb is dhyana or meditation, mentioned earlier. This is an unbroken flow of thought
toward God. The final limb is *samadhi* or the state of
complete absorption.

In one of the Upanishads we find this passage:
"The supreme heaven shines in the lotus of the heart;
they enter there who struggle and aspire. Retire into
solitude; seat yourself on a clean spot, and in erect
posture, with the head and neck in a straight line. Be
indifferent to the world." I remember one of the disciples of Sri Ramakrishna saying: "When you go to
meditate, forget even the Ramakrishna Mission. It is
just God and you."

And, continues the Upanishad, "Control all the
sense objects; bow down in devotion to your guru,
then enter the lotus of the heart, and there meditate on
the presence of Brahman, the Infinite, the Blissful."

Mysticism—True and False

THE great seer-philosopher, Shankara, once sketched a pen-and-ink drawing of a guru seated under a tree with his disciples surrounding him. The master was young and the disciples were old, and they were seated in silence. The disciples were old because our doubts, superstitions, and *karmas* are also old, as are the deeds and the effects of them which we carry from birth to death. The master is young because the truth of God, though ancient, is at the same time ever youthful and ageless.

Sri Ramakrishna tells a parable concerning a disciple who came to a teacher to study and learn about God. The disciple said, "Sir, teach me about God." The guru remained silent. Again the disciple asked the same question, and again the master said nothing. But when he asked the question the third time, the guru replied, "But I am teaching you, can't you see? His name is silence."

This truth—that in silence God becomes revealed in the hearts of the disciples and all doubts disappear—many of us witnessed for ourselves as we sat in the presence of our own Master, Swami Brahmananda, who was a direct disciple of Sri Ramakrishna. On occasion he would remain completely silent in the company of others, or talk about very casual things. But when these people left his presence, their problems were solved. And when we, his disciples, sat near him we felt that it was so very easy to find God; as though he were like a fruit in the palm of the hand.

This is what we call mysticism. The means by which that Reality, the ultimate truth of God, can be revealed in the hearts of each and every individual. And what is that ultimate Reality? It can best be defined in the words of the Upanishads: "The eternal amongst the noneternals of life; the highest abiding joy in the midst of the fleeting pleasures of life." And when this eternal truth becomes revealed within your own heart, then fulfillment comes into your life. Scriptures and gospels exist; you may read, study, and memorize them, even quote them glibly. But within your own heart, darkness and ignorance will still remain. God *is*. What is the proof? Proof is not the authority of the scriptures merely or words of the teacher. Proof lies in the fact that it is possible for you to *experience* God. For until you experience him for yourself, the truth of his existence will always be uncertain; doubts will continue to remain.

Unfortunately, in the West a great many ministers say that no one can see God. They tell us only to have faith. (Many of them are even denying the existence of God!) But to really have faith in God, I must know him. I must see him. Let me give you an illustration. There was once a young man by the name of Naren— later to become known as Swami Vivekananda— who doubted the existence of God. He said to himself that in order for me to believe in God's existence I must see him; the truth of his Being must be revealed to me. He went to various priests and holy men and asked them all the same question: "Sir, have you seen

God?" None of them could give him a satisfactory answer. Then he came, at long last, to Sri Ramakrishna and asked him: "Sir, have you seen God?"

And for the first time he was told: "Yes, I have seen him. I have seen him more directly, more distinctly than I now see you before me."

"Can you show him to me?"

"Yes, I can," Ramakrishna answered. For it was possible for him to grant that vision by only a touch. And not only a touch. I have, myself, heard from one of the disciples of Ramakrishna how this disciple was once seated under a tree trying to meditate. But his mind was distracted. Then, all at once, he saw Ramakrishna standing before him, gazing at him, and the disciple went into *samadhi*.

Did not Christ say: "Be thou whole!" They say Christ healed people, that he performed miracles. But did he come only to heal or perform miracles? No. (I am reminded of a statement by the French philosopher Rousseau: "Dispense with the miracles and the whole world will fall at the feet of Jesus Christ." And it is certain that a Hindu India would appreciate Christ more if miracles were not attributed to him.) Christ came to give eternal life, to give perfection, wholeness. But we cannot understand the scriptures or the teachings of these great ones unless and until we struggle for ourselves to find God. We must strive to realize the truth of God for ourselves. Then a new meaning comes to us. Whenever Sri Ramakrishna was asked how to find God, his answer would invariably be: "Yearn for him with a longing heart." This desire for God, this realization that he is the treasure of life is arrived at through discrimination. We begin to see that in the midst of all the fleeting pleasures of life there is an abiding truth, an abiding joy. And even if a little desire arises for God, that desire can be intensified through spiritual disciplines and struggle. Sri Ramakrishna used to say, "There is fire in the fuel. But just to believe that fuel has this potential is not enough. One must first light the fire and cook a meal over it! Then, and only then, will your hunger be satisfied."

WE MUST be convinced that no human being will ever be lost. Each man, woman, and child will, in some life or other, attain to that Reality. We read in one of the Upanishads: "Blessed is he who attains the truth of God in this life; otherwise, it is his greatest calamity." Why? Because he will be born again. He will have to be born once more and endure all this suffering— pleasure and pain, joy and sorrow—until God is known. We should remember this one principle of spiritual discipline, expressed by Christ in his Sermon on the Mount: "Blessed are the pure in heart, for they shall see God." (And yet today they teach, in the name of Christ, that no man can see God!) What did Christ mean by this—that the pure in heart shall see God? Did he mean that man will see God only after death? But is not the kingdom of heaven within you, here and now? Can you not enter that kingdom of God now, in this very life?

It is very easy to use this term, "purity of heart." Yet, what does it mean? Yearning for God. You see, you try to think of God, but because you are not interested in him your mind is distracted. There is a quotation which goes: "When the food* is pure, the heart becomes pure. When the heart becomes pure, then

* In this context, food means whatever we gather through the doors of the senses. In other words, we have to learn to cover everything with the presence of God.

there is constant recollectedness of God." That is the sign of a pure heart—constant recollectedness! And when that comes, there follows *prajna*: illumined knowledge of God. That is the simple truth. And prajna is the same as *samadhi*, *nirvana*, or *turiya*; all are names to describe Transcendental Consciousness. When you meditate, there is still duality; but in Transcendental Consciousness, there is no meditation. It is an experience.

This experience is indefinable and inexpressible. Though it is not communicable in so many words, it can be transmitted. Sri Ramakrishna and Christ could transmit this power by touch; others of us do not have that power. We transmit spirituality in a different way by pointing out to you the methods and means—the ways. One of these ways is through the power of the word given to you at initiation. Thus, the power is transmitted in seed form, and it is you who must nurture it through the practice of disciplines. Only then will this power grow into a tree and bear fruit.

Why are we unable to communicate the transcendental experience? Because it is absolute. There is nothing in it that can be related and understood. Sri Ramakrishna gave the illustration of a little girl who asked her elder sister what it was like to be married. "Wait until you grow up," answered the sister, "then when you are married yourself you will understand what it is like." Nothing can really be explained, she tells her sister, until you have a husband for yourself. Only then will you know.

We also hear of mystics who have described their experiences. They may say, "I see a blissful light. The world has disappeared. Waves of bliss are striking me." Or they may have a vision of their Chosen Ideal. But these are still not the highest experiences. If you stop there, progress ceases. My Master, Swami Brahmananda, once told us: "Light, more light, more light. Is there any end to it?"

This reminds me of an incident. A friend of mine once went to practice austerities and meditation in the Himalayas. After a period of three months he wrote me that he had attained samadhi. I happened to be with my Master at the time, so I told him about my friend's letter, and the fact that he claimed to have attained samadhi. Maharaj said: "What? I saw him some ten days ago and happened to notice his eyes. He has not attained samadhi. He may have experienced some light, perhaps, and thought that to be samadhi." Then Maharaj added: "Do you know what it means to have samadhi? All the knots of the heart become loosened; all ignorance vanishes, all doubts cease, all the effects of past deeds are erased. No longer is there desire for anything else. One becomes completely desireless, because he finds fulfillment in the eternal Reality."

IT IS through the mystic experience alone that true fulfillment comes. Otherwise, there will always be a lack within us. You may have all the wealth of the world at your command, and all the enjoyments which it can purchase—still within your heart there will be a sense of emptiness. In truth, God dwells within each and every heart, and until we discover him, until he becomes revealed to us, there will always be this feeling of a lack.

Still, one may say: is it not enough to be good, to be a moral, ethical humanist? Why bother finding God? In fact, Matthew Arnold once defined religion as "morality touched by emotion." But is this so easy? Is it so simple to become moral without the ideal of finding

God, without loving God? What is morality? It is to become selfless, totally selfless; to become egoless. And how can that be possible unless we find fulfillment in God?

Recently I read an article by a Christian minister who compared the relative contributions of an atheist and a Christian to the Viet Nam war. He said that the Christian went to war because he loved mankind as Christ did; but the atheist only loved him as man. It sounds wonderful to have such love for mankind, to love man as Christ loved us. But those who believe they love man in this way are only fooling themselves. Is it possible to love mankind as Christ loved us until we become absorbed in the love of Christ? Until we know and realize and experience how Christ loved? Have we any real idea how much Christ loved us? Have we ever seen him or felt his love?

In order for us to experience the real love of Christ we must become Christ-intoxicated. I hesitate to use the word God, for it appears that his name is no longer popular! God is dead, they say. But it is only in this Christ-intoxicated state that you will be able to know how Christ loved us. And only after that experience will you possess that love for others. Others talk about the way Christ loved us, but we do not love God that way. And these people themselves cannot live in harmony with one another. Husband and wife are unable to live in peace together, and yet they want to do good to mankind! "Man, no doubt, is the measure of all things; only his nature contains and reflects every level of reality from matter to spirit." Man is a physical being, a mental being, and a spiritual being. He can be any of them depending on whether he regards life from a physical, mental, or spiritual standpoint. The truth, however, is that although man has a body and mind, he is basically Spirit. This often is learned only after much experience in life, but learn it we must. We must tell ourselves: "I am God-divine. Mind and body are given me in order that I may use them as a means to unfold the Godhead within."

LET US say something further about mystic visions and the ultimate experience. Just as man consists of body, mind, and spirit, similarly there is the physical universe, the subtle universe, and the causal universe. Beyond that is what we call Brahman. Now, as in the physical universe we experience sight, hearing, taste, and so on, the psychic universe as well contains these sensory qualities. There one will hear sounds and see light. But mark! There is a difference between this light and the vision of spiritual light. The great yogi, Patanjali, the father of Indian Yoga philosophy, wrote about these psychic phenomena. He said that such powers and visions may be obtained by birth, by drugs, through the power of words, by the practice of austerity, or concentration. It is possible, therefore, to have "visions" through the use of drugs, but *only psychic, never spiritual visions.* India has known about such things for centuries; and there are those who do use such drugs there. But we generally consider them degenerates.

What is the test of spirituality? "Ye shall know them by their fruits." Therefore, we find that after the effects of these drugs have worn off, the user is the same man—if not worse. Their use can be extremely dangerous. Most important, they have caused no spiritual transformation. True, the senses become intensified under the influence of these drugs, the world "lights up," as it were; inanimate objects, pictures, and so forth, appear living. And there is an appearance, an awareness, that this is an experience of God. But it is not God. Because when God is realized your life is changed. You are no longer the same person. As Swami Vivekananda once said: "If a fool goes into samadhi, he comes out a wise man; but if a fool goes to sleep a fool, he still wakes up a fool." We can compare this sleep to the drug experience. Furthermore, though the users of such drugs think their ego is lost, in reality it has increased. Therefore, we see that psychic visions and powers, rather than assisting in spiritual growth, only serve to obstruct it.

It is important to remember that one of the great dangers which can arise from the use of drugs is that control over them can easily be lost. Should psychic powers come, there is always the temptation to use them; and through surrendering to such powers, all spiritual progress is stopped. It takes great strength, sometimes, to give up these powers. Let me tell you an incident from my own experience.

Once, when I was a young boy, our neighbor had a so-called holy man as his guest. This man had the rather unusual power of being able to create, upon your touching his toe, whatever fragrance you might wish. You only had to think of jasmine, rose, the smell of a lotus, or even a disagreeable smell, and the odor would invade your nostrils! I was quite excited about this. However, there was an old man present who watched me for a time and then said to me: "My boy, obtain a copy of Swami Vivekananda's *Raja Yoga*, and on page such-and-such you will find a description of these powers. You will also find that all spiritual progress is blocked for those who use them."

WHAT, then, is true mysticism? True mysticism is the conviction that God can be seen; that he can be directly known and realized; and that to have this realization is the only purpose in life. If we go to the very source of any religion, leaving aside theological dogma, we will find this same insistence on personal experience. Christ said, "Ye shall know the truth, and the truth shall make you free."

Mysticism has no creed, no theory, no dogma. It says that you can see God, talk with him, have a unitive knowledge of the Godhead. There have been mystics in all ages, and there will be mystics in ages to come. For it is the mystic, the saint to whom God has revealed himself, who keeps the truth of the scriptures alive.

But is the mystic experience, samadhi, so easy to attain? My Master said: "No, it is not a simple matter to experience God. One must practice, practice, practice." Samadhi is of two kinds: lower and higher. In the lower samadhi a sense of ego is still retained. You remain as the witness, though passive. In the higher kind of samadhi, ego totally disappears. There is no feeling, no emotion in that highest union. It is beyond all states of consciousness. But as one returns from the samadhi, one may live in two "states," as it were. That is, one can live in and experience this world, but at the same time be fully aware that it is not a real world, but only an appearance behind which he sees that there is only one Reality—Brahman. Or one can see all beings and things as Brahman. All is Brahman. To know and experience that Reality is the goal of the true mystic.

Know Thy Self

He who knows Brahman attains the supreme goal. Brahman is the abiding reality, he is pure knowledge, and he is infinity. He who knows that Brahman dwells within the lotus of the heart becomes one with him and enjoys all blessings.

Taittiriya Upanishad

EVERYONE'S life in this world is centered round the self. Each one of us lives in a little world of our own making. We refer to "my family," "my husband," "my wife," "my children," or "my country," "I desire this or that," and so forth. Of course, there is no need to prove that "I exist." Descartes, the father of modern Western philosophy, tried to establish the existence of self by his famous dictum: *Cogito, ergo sum*—"I think, therefore I exist." But to the Hindu logician, this is a roundabout proof. For he will answer by saying: "Before asking for proof of the existence of your self, *you have to exist*. It is self-evident. No proof is needed."

The main point to consider is this: "How many inquire into the nature of this self? Who am I? What am I? Who possesses a family or who desires to achieve this or that?" This must be our first and vital inquiry if we claim to be intellectual human beings apart from the lower animals or beasts.

And as this inquiry into what I am arises in us, there comes inevitably the question: "What, after all, is the purpose of life and living?" With this question we are again forced to confront the ultimate or eternal value of life.

Therefore, whether we will it or not, as we begin to seriously consider what the true nature of the self is, or what the eternal value of life is, we have to be philosophers or spiritually oriented people.

Strange as it may seem, what Christ called the kingdom of God, Vedanta calls *swaraj*, the kingdom of Self. For, as Christ also points out, the kingdom of heaven is not anything outside of ourselves, but *within*. Hence, we find the admonition by Christ "Seek ye first the kingdom of heaven" and in the Upanishads, "Know the Self alone; give up all vain talks."

"Seek ye first the kingdom of God and everything else shall be added unto you." Its simple meaning is that if we seek first the kingdom of God, there will be awakened in us love and compassion for all beings, and there will arise in our hearts an abiding happiness. But how often this wonderful teaching of Christ has been misunderstood. Many interpret "everything else" as health, success, prosperity, and so forth—the wordly things that are ephemeral. I do not mean to say, however, that we have to neglect these things. Surely we need health, we need economic stability, and we need to satisfy some of our legitimate human aspirations and human desires, however transitory they may be. (Not everyone is suited for monastic life—at least not until, perhaps, some of these desires are satisfied.) But these have to be the means and not the ends by themselves. We must never forget that the ultimate value of life is to attain that which is eternal—the kingdom of God or the kingdom of Self—while here, living on earth. As the Upanishads emphatically declare: "... here and now; not after the death of the body."

If, on the other hand, we forget the ultimate value of life, we shall only desire power, acquisition, and mastery over others. Unfortunately, many persons equate greatness with this possession of extensive wealth, power, or influence. But when we make worldly goods a means toward the attainment of the ultimate Reality, we shall seek to possess such virtues as self-control, moderation, openness, gentleness, unselfishness, and so forth.

Before I go any further, however, let me point out some basic differences between philosophy in the West and philosophy in the East, and the religion of the West and the religion of the East—though we must remember there is really no difference in the religions of the West and of the East if we go to their sources. They teach the same truth, though in different languages. The difference between East and West only appears when we examine what is being taught in the West now in the name of religion.

Philosophy in the West is a way of thinking, and attempts are made to reach the unknown—God or ultimate Reality—by a process of reasoning from what is known or experienced by the senses. On the other hand, in the East the word philosophy is called in Sanskrit *darshana*; that is, the vision or *experience* of the ultimate Reality. Ultimate Truth, the eternal value of life, cannot be comprehended intellectually or merely through the process of reasoning from the data given to us by our senses. For instance, the great Western

42

philospher Hegel apparently proved by his process of reasoning the existence of an absolute Reality. But isn't this only an *idea* of Reality which he has proved to exist? And what guarantee is there that his idea of the Absolute corresponds to Reality itself? Philosophers of the Western schools are not necessarily, therefore, wise men; wise are those who have *experienced* that ultimate Reality—call it God, or Self, or Brahman—names do not matter. I shall discuss this in detail later.

This same sort of thinking applies to the religion of the East as well as to that of the West; that is to say, to be spiritual one must experience the Truth for oneself. And herein lies the primary difference between the religion of the East and the contemporary religion of the West. Though all religions worth the name of religion are based upon revelation (that is, direct experience of the Truth), we find that now greater stress is laid upon authority. No emphasis is placed upon experiencing Truth for one's self. The Roman Catholic, for example, must accept the authority of the Church and Pope, whether or not his conscience or reason refuses such obedience. And beyond the authority of the Church or Pope lies the authority of the Book, the Bible. He must believe in every word of the Bible as the word of God. Have *faith* and you will attain eternal felicity in heaven, he is told. No wonder there is turmoil in every church today! Young people are questioning the authority of the church or of the scriptures, and with good reason.

In a sense, this is a propitious sign for the future, though at the present moment youth appears to be moving towards chaos by their rebellion. This is because of the lack of true leadership. I believe this phase is temporary. Why? Because we find that despite their rebelliousness, there is a genuine inquiry amongst some of them to come to a true understanding of religion.

WHAT did Christ teach and insist upon? "Seek and ye shall find"; "Knock and the door shall be opened unto you"; "Ye shall know the truth and the truth shall make you free." I can quote many such words of Christ to prove that he wanted each one of us to realize or experience the truth of God for ourselves. The religion of the East never forgot this ideal—the ideal of realizing God for oneself. Almost all the great teachers point out that scriptures are not the only proof of the existence of God, but that it is one's personal experience which serves as the real proof.

First of all, we should remember that philosophy or religion (Vedanta makes no distinction between them) is experience. And what is this ultimate experience of the Truth of God? In this connection, let me describe the supreme Truth as it is taught in Vedanta.

There are four Vedas. Each of these Vedas has a sacred dictum which gives the ultimate truth. These four dicta are: "Thou art That," "This Atman is Brahman," "Pure Consciousness is Brahman," and "I am Brahman." It is evident that though these four statements are distinct, they will have the same basic meaning—the identity of Atman and Brahman. But this, however, can only be a matter of experience.

For purposes of our discussion, let us consider the meaning of one of these statements, "Thou art That," the one most commonly known to Western readers. In their literal, superficial meaning, Brahman (which refers to That) and Atman (Thou, or the individual self) have opposite attributes, like the sun and the glowworm, the king and his servant, the ocean and the well. But their real identity is established when they

44

are understood in their true perspective; that is, only when experience is gained, not in a superficial sense, but by transcending the three states of consciousness— waking, dreaming, and dreamless sleep.

Brahman may refer to the Personal God, the ruler of *maya* and the creator of the universe, and the Atman may refer to the individual soul, associated with *avidya* or ignorance. Thus regarded, they possess opposite attributes. But this apparent opposition is caused by ignorance. It is not real, but superimposed. Let me quote to you some beautiful passages from the *Mundaka Upanishad*:

Like two birds of golden plumage, inseparable companions, the individual soul and the Immortal Self are perched on the branches of the self-same tree. The former tastes of the sweet and bitter fruits of the tree; the latter, tasting of neither, calmly observes.

The individual self, deluded by forgetfulness of his identity with the Divine Self, bewildered by his ego, grieves and is sad. But when he recognizes the worshipful Lord as his own true Self, and beholds his glory, he grieves no more.

When the seer beholds the effulgent one, the Lord, the Supreme Being, then transcending both good and evil, and free from impurities, he unites himself with him.

WHAT is this ego, the individual self—the ideas of "I," "me," and "mine"? Due to ignorance (which, in a sense, is universal) there has arisen in us the identification of the Atman, the true Self with the non-Atman, the sheaths or coverings of Self. According to Hindu psychology there are five such coverings of the Atman: the first is the body or *physical covering*. Any intelligent and discriminative man knows that he is not this

45

physical body. For the body is subject to change. And yet ignorance is so deep and universal that we identify ourselves with this body in our day-to-day activities in the empirical world.

The second covering of the Atman is called the *vital covering*. It is made up of the vital force and the organs by which actions are performed.

Next, the mind, together with the organs of perception, forms the *mental covering*.

Fourth, the discriminative faculty with its power of intelligence is known as the *covering of intellect*.

What is known in Western psychology as mind is described by Eastern psychology according to the different *functions* of the mind—such as mind (the receiving faculty), intellect (the discriminative faculty), and ego (the knower or experiencer). There is, therefore, a great distinction between Western and Eastern psychology with regard to the mind. In the West, intelligence is said to be an inherent character of the mind itself. But in the East, mind by itself is non-intelligent. True intelligence or Pure Consciousness, which is the Atman, is reflected upon the mind and makes it *appear* intelligent. As for instance, a piece of iron placed in fire becomes hot. Its nature is not inherently hot.

Because of this confusion some Western philosophers and psychologists are at a loss to explain the unconscious state of the mind. As the English philosopher John Locke once declared: "Every drowsy nod explodes the theory of self." (Mind is generally identified with the soul or self.) Furthermore, Locke says: "If the soul in a perfectly dreamless sleep thinks, feels, wills nothing, is the soul then at all, and if it is, how is it? How often has the answer been given that if this could happen, the soul would have no being. Why have we not the courage to say that as often as this happens, the soul is not." Another distinguished Western thinker, George Berkeley, says, "In sleep and trances the mind exists not—there is no time, no succession of ideas— to say that mind exists without thinking is a contradiction."

A Vedantist, however, will answer: Mr. Brown, after a sound sleep, continues to be the same Mr. Brown, since his experiences unite themselves to the system which existed at the time when he went to sleep. They link themselves to his thoughts and do not "fly" to any others. This continuity of experience requires us to admit a permanent Self underlying all contents of consciousness. As we read in the *Katha Upanishad*: "He through whom man experiences the sleeping or waking states is the all-pervading Self. Knowing him one grieves no more."

I have already mentioned the four coverings of the Self. There is a fifth one, called the *covering of bliss*. This covering is revealed to us in the state of deep sleep. It is called the covering of bliss because it is the covering closest to the blissful Atman. But this covering, also, is a creation of our ignorance.

The Atman is beyond the five coverings. In order to realize our true Being, the Atman, which is one with Brahman, we have to go beyond the three states of consciousness, waking, dreaming, and dreamless sleep, and reach turiya or the Fourth, which, in the language of the yogis, is called samadhi. The Buddhists call this same consciousness nirvana, and Christ refers to it as "birth in Spirit."

BEFORE I explain what this experience is and how to attain it, I must mention in passing that the truth that the Atman or the Self is Brahman is not unique

47

to Vedanta. The mystics, those great ones of all the religions, have said the same thing, for they have realized the same truth in themselves. The Sufis' dictum "*Anul Hak*" means "I am He." In *Romans* 8:16 we read: "The spirit itself beareth witness with our spirit that we are the children of God; and if children, then heirs; heirs of God and joint heirs with Christ."

"God's light," one Christian mystic says, "dwells in the Self; it shines alike in every living being and one can see it with one's mind steadfast."

And Meister Eckhart: "Some there are so simple as to think of God as if He dwelt there and of themselves as being here. It is not so. God and I are one."

We should not, however, understand these statements to mean that *a part* of God dwells in each one of us. The truth is that the Infinite cannot be divided into finite parts. The one infinite Being dwells everywhere in its infinite aspect.

Let us see what our modern scientists have to say on this point. Science has dematerialized matter; the ultimate substance is energy or light, and this light is the light of Consciousness. And as the famous physicist and biologist Erwin Schrodinger declared, "Consciousness is never experienced in the plural, only in the singular . . . a plurality is merely a series of different aspects of this one thing produced by deception [the Indian maya]." And this consciousness, which is the Self or Brahman, has been experienced ultimately in the transcendental state by the mystics and seers of all ages and countries. That is the one supreme goal of human life.

As already stated, this is a matter of experience. Though we may believe in the words of the scriptures or be intellectually convinced of the truth of God, the immortality of the Self, or oneness of the Self with

Brahman, yet our ignorance is not removed. As the seer-philosopher Shankara clearly pointed out: "Scriptures are not the only authority for the acceptance of the truth of Self; but one must have one's own personal experience." Study of the scriptures is fruitless if one does not make an attempt to realize Brahman and ultimately experience him in one's own soul. In the *Mahabharata* we read: "He who has no personal knowledge, but has heard many things cannot understand the scriptures, even as a spoon has no idea of the taste of the soup."

Thus the paramount urge in every intelligent human being should be to make every effort to realize the Self or God. There can be no joy in the universe for one who lives within the boundary of his empirical ego. Swami Brahmananda, my Master, once said to me, pointing to his own heart, "He who finds him here [that is, within his own heart] finds him everywhere. If he does not seek and find him there, he can find him nowhere." He is neither to be found in temples, nor in churches, on earth nor in heaven. You may pray for him in churches or temples, and you may go to the Himalayas or the Gobi desert in search of him. However, at long last, you will find him as the nearest of the near, in your own Self, the reality of your life, body, and soul.

Now the fundamental question is how to realize the Self; how to experience and know the true nature of the Atman as one with Brahman. As already stated we have to go beyond the three states of consciousness. Of course, it is evident that this cannot be attained through the ordinary means of knowledge—that is, knowledge gained from direct perception by the five ordinary senses or inferred from the data they provide. This knowledge of Atman-Brahman can only be attained by the subtle, supersensuous power of yoga. However, before I explain the means to its attainment, let me state the effects of such knowledge. (For, as the saying goes, "A tree is known by its fruits.") A short verse in the *Mundaka Upanishad* states: "The heart is tied into a knot by its ignorance. When this knot is loosed, all doubts are dissolved, all evil effects of deeds are destroyed."

What are the means? Shankara, following the teachings of the Upanishads, states, "The disciple must hear the truth of the Atman, and reflect upon it, and meditate upon it constantly. Thus the wise man reaches that highest state, in which consciousness of subject and object is dissolved away and the infinite unitary consciousness alone remains—and he knows the bliss of nirvana while still living on earth."

The first and most important thing is to be a disciple and hear the truth of God from the lips of a guru—an illumined soul. This is the one condition for traveling the path; one needs the help of a guide. In Vedanta, this transmission of truth is known as *diksha* or initiation; in Christianity, it is known as baptism.

In this connection, let me quote the words of Christ: "Except a man be born of water and of the Spirit, he cannot enter the kingdom of God." In other words, one needs to be baptised or initiated first by an illumined soul; then only can one be born in Spirit; that is to say, be illumined in the knowledge of God. We find for instance, one of Christ's disciples, Nicodemus doubting the possibility of this. But Christ rebukes him, and ultimately states: "That whosoever believeth in him should not perish, but have everlasting life."

Yes, according to the Vedanta, in order to "have everlasting life" we need to have faith in the words of the guru and in the words of the scriptures. And my Master added that you must also have faith in yourself. If others have realized God, so I also can realize him. We find another interesting correspondence with Vedantic teachings in the third chapter of the *Gospel according to St. John*: "And no man hath ascended up to heaven, but he that came down from heaven, even the Son of man which is in heaven."

Is not this a clear statement from the lips of Christ that each man in his true being is divine—one has to have descended from heaven in order to be able to ascend. This truth we must hear from the lips of a guru—an illumined soul.

Then reflect upon this truth. That is to say, through reasoning upon it, one must come to the conviction that the ego, the individual soul, is not the Atman— is not divine. It is ignorance that makes us identify ourselves with the *coverings* of the Atman.

Lastly we must meditate upon the truth of the At- man-Brahman. What this meditation is, is beautifully explained by a few words in the *Katha Upanishad*: "When all the senses are stilled, when the mind is at rest, when the intellect wavers not—that say the wise, is the highest state. This calm of the senses and the mind has been defined as yoga. He who attains it is freed from delusion. With mind illumined by the power of meditation, the wise know him, the blissful, the immortal."

In this connection I wish to also quote from the *Bhagavad-Gita*:

When can a man be said to have achieved union with Brahman? When his mind is under perfect control, and freed from all desires, so that he becomes absorbed in the Atman, and nothing else. "The light of a lamp does not flicker in a windless place," that is the simile which describes a yogi of one-pointed mind, who meditates upon the Atman. When through the practice of yoga the mind ceases its restless movements, and becomes still, he realizes the Atman. Thus he knows that infinite happiness which can be realized by the purified heart but is beyond the grasp of the senses.

From the above quotations, it is evident that to have one-pointedness of the mind towards God, or "to pray to God unceasingly" one must acquire purity of heart. The Upanishads declare unequivocally that only by the pure in heart does the Reality become known. This truth, too, is taught by Christ in his famous saying, "Blessed are the pure in heart, for they shall see God." Thus purity is the bedrock upon which the whole of the spiritual life rests. Ramanuja, one of the great devotees of India and the propounder of the philosophy of qualified nondualism, prepared a list of qualities conducive to purity. These may be considered to be taught in every religion. They are: truthfulness, sincerity, doing good to others without any gain to one's own self, not injuring others by words, thoughts, or deeds and not coveting others' goods.

In the *Chandogya Upanishad* we discover a beautiful truth regarding the way to attain purity. "When the food is purified, the heart becomes pure." This is the first condition—to purify the food. Food, of course, does not mean simply what we eat, but the knowledge or experience we gather through the doors of the senses. How is that knowledge or experience to be purified? Shankara states that though we may move amongst the objects of senses, we must learn not to have any "attachment or aversion for them." And in the Gita we read, "The attraction and aversion which the senses feel for different objects are natural. But we must not give way to such feelings; they are obstacles."

At the same time the Gita points out that "a man who renounces certain physical actions but still lets his mind dwell on the objects of his sensual desire, is deceiving himself. He can only be called a hypocrite. The truly admirable man controls his senses by the power of the will. All his actions are disinterested. All are directed along the path to union with Brahman."

Now to come back to the *Chandogya Upanishad*: "When the food is purified, the heart becomes pure, and when the heart becomes pure, there comes constant recollectedness of the Reality and thus all the bondages of ignorance become loosed and the Truth becomes revealed."

So it ultimately comes to this: the one test of purity of heart is that the mind runs spontaneously towards God, and never ceases in its yearning for Him. My Master used to teach us to practice recollectedness of God while eating, walking, or sitting. His one insistence was to "practice, practice, practice!" Thus, through practice and dedicated struggle we will at last know and experience God, who is none other than our very Self.

FAITH

SWAMI PRABHAVANANDA

In the College Standard dictionary we find this definition of faith: "The assent of the mind or understanding to the truth of what God has revealed." This definition expresses the Western attitude towards faith: the mind must accept the truth of God as he reveals it. Now let us see how the Vedantist philosopher Shankara defines faith. He says: "A firm conviction, based upon intellectual understanding, that the teachings of the scriptures and of one's master are true—this is called by the sages the faith which leads to realization of the Reality."

There are differences between the Western and Eastern conceptions of faith, differences in interpretation and emphasis. But it is more important that we try to understand the principle which is common to both points of view, and which is accepted by all the great religions of the world—this universal principle being the insistence upon faith in the scriptures, because the scriptures contain the revealed words of God.

But what exactly are the scriptures? And why are they regarded as authoritative? Before we inquire further into these questions, we must understand that three kinds of proof exist. The first kind of proof is sense perception. I see an object before me; my senses perceive it. That is one kind of proof. The second kind of proof is inference. An inference is a truth drawn from another which is admitted to be true. For instance, I see smoke, therefore I conclude that there must be a fire; because from past observation I have learned that wherever there is smoke there is fire. And the third kind of proof is revelation—transcendental knowledge, or superconscious vision.

Although it may sound strange to Western ears, I must point out here that two kinds of truth exist. One kind of truth is perceived by the senses; and the other kind of truth, which cannot be perceived by the senses, is perceived through the subtle supersensuous power of yoga.

Take, for instance, the truths of God, soul, and immortality. Nobody can perceive these truths through the senses. Once a doctor, trying to disprove the immortality of the soul, remarked that he had seen hundreds of people die, yet he never saw a soul come out of a body. Obviously, such an argument is meaningless, because no believer in spiritual concepts claims that the soul can be seen with physical eyes. Religious truths can be perceived only supersensuously, through revelation.

Now, what are the scriptures? They are revelations given to sages, seers, or divine incarnations like Christ, Buddha, or Ramakrishna. Furthermore, these great teachers are not unique in the sense that they alone were able to perceive the truth of God. You and I, anyone who develops that supersensuous power, may do so. And that is the point we must try to understand. Why should we have faith in the words of the scriptures? Because they are revelation. The truth of God was revealed to Christ, Krishna, Moses, Mohammed, and other world teachers. And these teachers have pointed out that every individual at a certain stage of spiritual unfoldment can experience this same truth.

As I have already mentioned, the truth of God cannot

be known by any means other than revelation. Of course we find that attempts have been made, and are still being made, to establish the existence of God by reasoning. But all such attempts are futile. For example, the great philosopher Hegel proves with logic and reason that an absolute reality exists. Other philosophers by the use of logic and reason can refute his arguments. But let us suppose that Hegel's arguments prevail. Nevertheless, what guarantee is there that his idea of the Absolute corresponds to the absolute reality which he tries to prove? What can a philosopher prove, after all? Only his *idea* of a reality, his *idea* of an Absolute. And that is why one often hears people say, "I don't believe in God." What is it that they do not believe in? Certain ideas of God, which do not appeal to them. Reason therefore, although it has an important place in spiritual life—as we shall see later —is insufficient to prove the existence of God. The only real proof of his existence is to see him.

You may ask, Supposing the truth of God was revealed to Christ, or Moses, or Ramakrishna; and supposing it is revealed to me—but what is the criterion of the truth of God? The criterion is that this truth is absolute. This means that it must be *trikala abadhittva*, not contradicted by time past, present, or future.

All other truths are known through the senses or through inference; and they are only relatively true. For instance, I see a table in front of me. It exists in the present; it did not always exist in the past, nor will it always exist in the future. Moreover, when the Reality is revealed to me, the table will disappear; and everything will be seen as Brahman.

Or take the dream experience. While we are dreaming, our dreams have a relative reality; but our dreams are contradicted by the waking experience. When we wake up, they vanish.

by Swami Prabhavananda

Brahman, the Pure Consciousness, is present in all three states of ordinary awareness—waking, dreaming and dreamless sleep. It is the ground of everything we experience in these three states. But Brahman in its total reality is experienced only in the transcendental consciousness. When we attain that consciousness, our waking experience also is contradicted. But the transcendental experience is never contradicted by any other experience. Therefore it has a greater reality than either sense perception or inference.

Is there any other criterion of transcendental knowledge? How can we distinguish, for instance, between transcendental truth and psychic phenomena? Before any revelation is recognized as genuinely transcendental, it must be related to *arthe anupalabdhe*—something which is otherwise unknown and unknowable.

If I have psychic power, for example, I can look at you and guess correctly how many dollars you have in your coat pocket. But that is not transcendental knowledge, because I can get this information in other ways. I can ask you how much money you have on you, or I can threaten you with a gun and search your coat pocket.

Transcendental revelation, on the other hand, is not a revelation of things normally perceived, nor of truths apprehended through the ordinary instruments of knowledge. And yet it must be universally understandable in relation to human experience, and must be communicable to us in human terms.

IN the Upanishads we read: "Brahman words cannot reveal; mind cannot reach; eyes cannot see. How then save through those who know him, can he be known?" We can learn of God only through those who have had direct experience of

God. This means faith in the scriptures, because the scriptures have been revealed to the seers and sages.

But according to Vedanta, faith in the scriptures is not enough. We must also have faith in the words of the guru, the living teacher. There must be living exemplars of the scriptural truths, otherwise the scriptures are misunderstood or become forgotten.

Even to believe in the words of the scriptures and of the guru is not enough. Our faith—as we read in Shankara's definition—must lead to the realization of God. Belief must be translated into action. This is true even in worldly matters. For a medical student to read and have faith in materia medica is not enough. He must become an intern in a hospital, and through personal experience with patients learn how to diagnose and prescribe. Similarly, reading the scriptures and believing in them is only the beginning of spiritual aspiration. One must experiment with the truth of God and experience it for oneself.

To quote the Upanishads again: "The truth of the Atman must be heard about, reasoned upon, and meditated upon." First, we must learn about the truth of the Atman, the Self within, from the scriptures and from the lips of a teacher who has experienced the truth himself.

The second step is reasoning. Having heard about the truth, we must not accept it blindly, without understanding it. We must test it, and question the teacher. Our reason must be satisfied. Although revelation is beyond and above reason, it does not contradict it. Thus Vedanta, though having its foundation in supernatural revelation, gives a legitimate place to reason.

The third step is meditation. Once we have become intellectually convinced of the truth of God, what will we do? We will want to realize it. Unless a man acts on the basis of his intellectual understanding, unless he tries to reach the transcendental consciousness, his faith is mere lip faith. Mohammed compared such a man to a donkey carrying a load of books.

In order to illustrate the inadequacy of mere scholarship, Sri Ramakrishna used to tell the following parable.

Some men were crossing the Ganges in a boat. Among them was a pandit who was proud of his learning. He was telling his fellow passengers how familiar he was with the six systems of philosophy. He questioned one of the men: "Do you know Vedanta?" "No, revered sir." "How about Sankhya and Yoga?" No, revered sir." "Haven't you read any philosophy at all?" "No, revered sir." When the boat reached the middle of the river, a storm arose. The boat was on the point of capsizing, when one of the passengers asked the pandit: "Sir, do you know how to swim?" "No," was his answer. Then the passenger remarked, "I don't know Sankhya or Yoga; but I do know how to swim."

Religion is very pragmatic. We must learn to swim— swim across this ocean of worldliness and reach the other shore, where we are safe, where we are freed from all limitations, and where there is no sorrow.

But the difficulty is that we have so little interest in God. Faith in him is rare. Emerson said: "There is faith in chemistry, in meat and wine, in wealth, in machinery, in the steam engine, galvanic battery, turbine wheels, sewing machines, and in public opinion, but not in divine causes." As the Gita puts it: "Who cares to seek for that perfect freedom? One man, perhaps, in many thousands." When Sri Ramakrishna told his young disciple Naren that few people have faith in God, the boy objected, saying that he knew many who were believers. Then Sri Ramakrishna replied: "Suppose a thief knows that just beyond the wall there is a great treasure. Would he rest quietly? No, he would struggle with all his might to get hold of it!"

The intensity of our struggle then is the test of our faith. We must practice spiritual disciplines; we must make repeated efforts to realize our true nature, which is divine, one with God. Ignorance of our divinity is an immediate experience, and another immediate experience—revelation, or supersensuous vision—is needed to dispel the ignorance.

The necessity of self-effort and practice is pointed out by Shankara: "A buried treasure is not uncovered by merely uttering the words 'Come forth.' You must follow the right directions, dig, remove stones and earth from above it, and then make it your own. In the same way, the pure truth of the Atman, which is buried under maya and the effects of maya, can be reached by meditation, contemplation, and other spiritual disciplines such as a knower of Brahman may prescribe—but never by subtle arguments."

Now what are the fundamental truths or principles upon which we must base our faith? First of all, we must have faith that *God is*. Even if we do not have this faith to begin with—if we are seekers after truth and follow certain spiritual disciplines, we will gradually become convinced of the existence of God.

Secondly, we should have the faith that *God can be realized*. Merely to be convinced that he exists is not enough. We must have the confidence: "Others have realized him, and so can I."

Finally, we must be convinced that *to realize God is the supreme goal of human existence*. Why? Because in God alone there is complete fulfillment.

What is the way to achieve this ultimate purpose of life? A Christian mystic pointed out: "God's light dwells in the

by Swami Prabhavananda

Self; it shines alike in every living being, and one can see it with one's mind steadied." And the Indian saint Ramprasad said: "Fix your heart in God, then love will awaken within; and faith is the root of all." How to steady the mind and fix the heart in God is explained in greater detail in the Gita: "Patiently, little by little, a man must free himself from all mental distractions with the aid of the intelligent will. He must fix his mind upon the Atman, and never think of anything else. No matter where the restless and unquiet mind wanders, it must be drawn back and made to submit to the Atman only."

You may fail many times in your efforts to direct the mind singly to God and to keep it in his presence. Don't become discouraged. With perseverance continue your spiritual practices. Sri Ramakrishna said: "Countless are the pearls lying hidden in the sea. If a single dive yields you none, do not conclude that the sea is without pearls. Similarly, if after practicing spiritual disciplines for a little while you fail to have the vision of God, do not lose heart. Practice the disciplines with patience, and at the proper time you are sure to obtain grace."

If you continue your practices patiently and faithfully, you will one day have a tangible feeling of the presence of God. Until you come to this stage, you may be troubled by the doubt that God really exists. Occasionally doubts arise even after God's presence has been experienced; but such doubts make the aspirant struggle harder and in this way further his spiritual growth. As the living presence of God is experienced, a sweetness is felt within, and love for God will grow in your heart. Then comes constant recollectedness of his presence. A current in your mind flows continually toward God. When you reach this stage of unfoldment, there arises *prajna*—illumination, or the vision of God.

Prior to illumination the kind of faith we have may be termed "working faith." This kind of faith is the root of spiritual life. But after illumination a different kind of faith comes—a lasting faith, which is the fruit of God-realization.

In this connection, I am reminded of something M., the compiler of Sri Ramakrishna's Gospel, told me many years ago, when I asked his blessings before leaving for America. On this occasion I inquired, "What is the greatest thing you achieved by coming to Sri Ramakrishna?" M.'s answer was: "Faith." As M. was an intimate disciple of Sri Ramakrishna and an illumined soul, I knew he meant the faith that follows God-vision.

My master, Swami Brahmananda, referred to this same kind of faith when he said, on his deathbed: "I am floating on a leaf of faith on the ocean of Brahman."

What is the nature of a man who has found this deeper faith? How does it manifest in him? In the sixth chapter of the Gita we find a description of the illumined soul and his state of attainment:

When, through the practice of yoga, the mind ceases its restless movements, and becomes still, he realizes the Atman. It satisfies him entirely. Then he knows that infinite happiness which can be realized by the purified heart but is beyond the grasp of the senses. He stands firm in this realization. Because of it he can never again wander from the truth of his being.

Now that he holds it he knows this treasure above all others: faith so certain shall never be shaken by heaviest sorrow. . . .

Released from evil, his mind is constant in contemplation. The way is easy. Brahman has touched him; that bliss is boundless.